Obsessed

breaking free from the things
that consume you

Hayley DiMarco

Revell

a division of Baker Publishing Group
www.RevellBooks.com

Hungry
Planet

Published by Revell
a division of Baker Publishing Group
P.O. Box 6287, Grand Rapids, MI 49516-6287
www.revellbooks.com

Printed in the United States of America

Library of Congress Cataloging-in-Publication Data
DiMarco, Hayley.
    Obsessed : breaking free from the things that consume you / Hayley
DiMarco.
        p.   cm.
    ISBN 978-0-8007-3306-3 (pbk.)
    1. Idolatry. 2. Obsessive-compulsive disorder—Religious aspects—
Christianity. I. Title.
    BV4627.I34D56 2012
    248.8'6—dc23   2012017993

Published in association with Christopher Ferebee, Literary Agent, Corona, California.

12 13 14 15 16 17 18   7 6 5 4 3 2 1

Contents

1. The Obsessed Soul 7

2. Obsessed with Loss 35

3. Obsessed with Gain 65

4. Obsessed with Relief 95

5. Obsessed with God 119

Notes 151

1

The Obsessed Soul

Things have become necessary to us, a development never originally intended. God's gifts now take the place of God, and the whole course of nature is upset by the monstrous substitution.

A. W. Tozer, *The Pursuit of God*

God must be all or he is nothing. God can't do all unless you expect him to do all. And you can't expect him to do it all until you are obsessed with him and him alone. No other obsession, no question, can come between you and your God.

Hayley DiMarco

O bsessed. Consumed. Controlled.
Devoted. Ruled.

The obsessed are undeterred.

They are unstoppable.

Nothing keeps them from the object of their obsession—not fire, not danger, not fear, not humiliation, nothing.

To be obsessed is to want one thing more than anything else.

To be consumed with thoughts of whatever obsesses you.

To be unable to walk away.

To be mastered and possessed by desire for the object of your obsession and the rewards for attaining it.

To be obsessed is to do all you can to serve your passion. Obsession is the fuel that can change lives for both good and bad. **Obsession determines destiny.** The obsessed are unparalleled in their ability to focus on and to achieve whatever they are fixated on. And because of that they are also unparalleled in their ability to change the world around them for the better or to mess it up royally.

The obsessed follow hard after their passion. They do this because of the great reward they are receiving or hoping to receive when they do. They have big goals, big dreams, and big hopes. They will put all their eggs in one basket, lay it all on the line, and go all in for the thing they love because they are convinced the payoff makes all the suffering and strain worth it.

The Fame of Obsession

Leonardo da Vinci was obsessed with sketching everything he thought, saw, or imagined. Amelia Earhart was obsessed with flying. Julia Child was obsessed with cooking. Florence Nightingale was obsessed with medicine.

Obsession is behind many of the famous accomplishments throughout time, even the biblical ones. When God told Abraham to kill his son, Abraham made preparations to do just that. He was so obsessed with one thing and one thing only—love for his God—that nothing could change his mind, not even the cries of his beloved son (see Gen. 22). Abraham was obsessed.

When Noah gave up everything else in his life to do something as crazy as building a huge ship in his front yard (see Gen. 6), the people laughed and jeered. They scorned him and doubted him. But for some fifty years[1] he continued building the monstrosity that made him look like a fool. He did what his God commanded, because he was consumed with God and God alone. Noah was obsessed.

Even though the apostle Paul had been beaten, shipwrecked, starved, and imprisoned because of his preaching, he wouldn't stop (see 2 Cor. 11:24–27). The only thing he lived for, breathed for, and even died for was Jesus. Paul was obsessed.

Obsessions are memorable, if only to the obsessed. Sold out devotion makes a difference, and no matter what the object, devotion will have its end in either good or evil. For many obsessed people, devotion has an ugly end. In dark lives like those of the criminally or neurotically obsessed, we see tragedy of epic proportions. The alcoholic's craving destroys his life and the lives of those he loves. The drug addict's habit does the same. The one fixated on stuff ends up with nothing. And the one who obsesses over love ends up alone. The degree and manner of obsession reveal a lot about the future of the obsessed. And the obsessed make history when their passion is all consuming.

Faith Is Obsessed

Obsession colors our lives, changes them, and directs them. That's why this issue is so important to God. In fact, *obsessed* would be an accurate descriptor of the Christian believer. Don't agree? Think obsession is only reserved for the few? You've got to think again, because Jesus made it clear when he said, "Love the Lord your God with *all* your heart and with *all* your soul and with *all* your strength and with *all* your mind, and your neighbor as yourself" (Luke 10:27).

These words epitomize the life of the obsessed: giving all of your heart, soul, mind, and strength to one thing. **You were made to be obsessed—obsessed with your Creator.** That is why obsession comes so naturally. It's how you are wired; it's what you were meant for. You were designed to love God with all your strength.

Without obsession, faith isn't possible. That's why Jesus had to push the subject further by saying, "None of you can be my disciples unless you give up everything" (Luke 14:33 GW). See, this love for God compels you to give up everything in favor of your one obsession. That's why Jesus says these hard-to-swallow words in Matthew 10:37: "The person who loves his father or mother more than me does not deserve to be my disciple. The person who loves a son or daughter more than me does not deserve to be my disciple" (GW). The one obsessed with God puts nothing before him—not even the people she loves.

Jesus has so much to say about this stuff, and he made a foundational statement when he told us that we can't have two obsessions: "No one can serve two masters. He will hate the first master and love the second, or he will be devoted to the first and despise the second" (Matt. 6:24 GW). The obsessed serves her master, and she cannot serve two masters. We can either be obsessed with God or something else. **If you claim two obsessions, then you are not truly obsessed with both. No one is obsessed part time.** Obsession is continual.

You were made
to be obsessed—

obsessed with your Creator.

Our Obsessed History

Those who have come before us who have been obsessed with God have laid the foundation of faith that we now stand on. Perhaps no one did this more than the apostle Paul, who spent the entire second half of his life writing the inspired words of the New Testament and preaching salvation to the masses. Like Paul, the truly obsessed can honestly say that "whether I eat or drink, or whatever I do, I do everything to the glory of God" (see 1 Cor. 10:31). He is their obsession.

The obsessed are convinced, like Paul, that they can do all things through Christ who strengthens them (see Phil. 4:13), and because of that they have changed the world. Just look at the obsessed believers throughout history. One example is Amy Carmichael, who was so devoted to the Father that as a teenager she became determined to change the lives of homeless and abused children around the world. Even though she suffered from a painful disease that would keep her in bed for sometimes a month at a time and often leave her temporarily blind, she still did all she could to get to the mission field. When her first application was rejected because of her health, she pushed on and tried again until someone accepted her.

While working in India, Amy discovered that little girls were being sold by their parents into temple prostitution, and she had to do something about it. She began to take in these girls to rescue them, even risking her own life to do it. Amy founded the Dohnavur Fellowship, which became a refuge for many girls, and even took in babies who were born while their moms were in prostitution. Her love for God gave her so much determination and drive that she worked for fifty-six years in India without ever taking a furlough.

Another obsessed believer was Hudson Taylor, who at nineteen knew he could trust God for all that he needed and so went on to found the China Inland Mission, serving the Chinese people in a way no one had done previously. Hudson loved God to obsession. He believed in living to serve others and not himself, so when he got to China he did something none of the other missionaries would do: he put on Chinese clothes and grew his hair long and put it into a ponytail to look like a native.

Hudson was so convinced that God could supply all of his needs that he never asked for support but only prayed that God would provide what he needed. And day by day, week by week, month by month, that's exactly what God did. Because of Hudson's obsession, no one who came to join his mission organization ever had a guaranteed salary or asked people for support, but they were called to ask God for what they needed. The organization grew radically. In 1881, Hudson asked God for another 70 missionaries by Christmas 1884, and he got 76. In 1886 he prayed for another 100 and got 102.

Hudson knew the value of the obsessed believer, so much so that he said this of his missionaries: "The stamp of men and women we need is such as will put Jesus, China, [and] souls first and foremost in everything and at every time—even life itself must be secondary."[2] Hudson's obsession knew no bounds!

Those who are obsessed with what they were born to be obsessed with—God himself—have hope, healing, and peace (see Matt. 8:17; John 14:27; Rom. 8:37). Their obsession never puts them to shame (see Rom. 10:11), never disappoints (see Rom. 5:5), and never leads them to destruction (see John 3:36). The one true obsession meant for all people is the answer to all that ails you. When you are obsessed with God, not even suffering can harm or deter you.

The Danger of Obsession

Unfortunately, obsessed isn't a term often used to describe the average believer today, at least not in a good way. It's most often used to describe some kind of glorious infatuation, destructive pleasure, or nasty habit that is difficult to break. The obsessed can't control themselves; they are so in love with the pleasure their obsession gives them that they are often powerless to deny it, and so they end up becoming a slave to the very thing that initially seemed to offer them so much freedom. That's because being obsessed always ultimately serves the obsession rather than the person who is obsessed.

When you devote yourself to, glorify, serve, and even worship the object of your affection and that object isn't a holy God, the results are dangerous. **You were designed to be obsessed with God, so when you are obsessed with anything or anyone other than God, that something or someone competes for the role of**

19

God in your life. Then you begin to serve, to honor, to meditate on, and to devote yourself to something that was never meant to receive your worship, and that's when obsession becomes dangerous.

Obsession is about being overly devoted or attached to something or someone. And out of that devotion comes worship. Worship requires things of the obsessed: it requires love, sacrifice, preoccupation, and service. **The worship you give your passion is the biggest danger in obsession.** Obsession creates a rival for God that demands as much attention and devotion as you give God, if not more.

Worship might sound like something you've only ever given to God, but truth be told, most of us have worshiped more than God in our lives. A lot of girls idolize musicians or actors. They research them, study them, hang pictures of them, cry before them, dream of them, pursue them, study them, worship them. Others worship success and put all their energy into getting things done, being the best, and making something of their lives.

Worship most often starts out as a response to the feelings the thing gives you. You love how you feel doing something, so you want to do it more and more, and pretty soon you adore that something or someone for how they make you feel. So feelings of love are often the beginning of worship. And while loving is a biblical command, the feelings of love generated by an obsession aren't the same thing. Biblical love is a response to a loving God. It involves giving grace to those who have hurt you; it expresses forgiveness, compassion, and service; and it isn't dependent on feelings. Those amazing feelings we first get when we begin to fall in love with our obsession aren't meant to turn into worship, but when they do, the obsessed begin to serve their feelings over their God. **You can serve your own pleasure or you can serve God, but you can't serve both.**

Worship involves sacrifice. In order to worship something, you must be willing to sacrifice for it, as you can see in Romans 12:1: "I encourage you to offer your bodies as living sacrifices, dedicated to God and pleasing to him. This kind of worship is appropriate for you" (GW). If you are sacrificing your body to something or someone other than God—if you sacrifice your nourishment for being thin, your health for taking drugs or overeating, your skin for cutting, or your heart for getting love—then you

You can serve your own pleasure or you can serve God, but you can't serve both.

are worshiping something other than God. The danger is easy to see here. When what you love or deeply desire demands the harsh treatment of your body, heart, or mind to the point of sin, then you end up destroying the temple of God in order to serve yourself.

Witnessing is an act of worship (see Rom. 15:16). When you spend any amount of your time talking about your obsession, getting others to see the beauty of it, the benefit of it, and the value of it, you are witnessing, and this is your act of worship. I know a girl who loves God but loves her boyfriend a little bit more. How do I know this? Because her boyfriend is all she talks about. She is always trying to tell me how amazing he is. Always telling me what special things he has done. Always bragging, always glorifying, always worshiping. And while this might just seem like a fun thing to do and a great way to feel good about the love of your life, it betrays a deeper story than that. It betrays an obsession, another god in her life. Since she talks about him more than she talks about the true God, I know the order of worship in her heart.

If you find yourself giving constant witness about a certain topic—working to convince others of something like the great things about a political view, a certain diet, a television show, or a way of living—then chances are you are obsessed. Your conversation says everything about your obsession.

Another danger of obsession is that it controls you—your thoughts, your feelings, even your time. The obsessed girl is managed by her obsession. She does everything she can to get to it, to experience it, to talk about it, and to live with it. She becomes a slave to the obsession. In 2 Peter 2:19 we learn that "you are a slave to whatever controls you" (NLT). Once you love something to the point of obsession you are no longer your own but have become a slave to your obsession. That's why addictions are so hard to break and obsessions are so hard to stop—because we are enslaved by them.

You might not even be aware of this kind of control in your life, but think about the things you do and why you do them. Is there any area in your life where you have given over control to something or someone else? Anything that you feel like you need so much that it controls all your thoughts? If you think about something almost all day, if it colors almost all your choices and your relationships, your conversations and your actions, then you are obsessed and controlled.

As a believer you were meant to live in freedom. We know this because of Galatians 5:1, which says, "Christ has freed us so that we may enjoy the benefits of freedom. Therefore, be firm in this freedom, and don't become slaves again" (GW). Unfortunately, **those obsessed with anything but God mistakenly believe that their earthly addiction is their answer to freedom**, but nothing could be further from the truth. The obsessed is a slave to her obsession. It controls her and puts her in bondage. It runs roughshod over her, telling her when to jump and just how high. Obsession is bondage, and bondage to anything or anyone other than Jesus is sin. "Do you not know that if you present yourselves to anyone as obedient slaves, you are slaves of the one whom you obey, either of sin, which leads to death, or of obedience, which leads to righteousness?" (Rom. 6:16). There are your two choices: you can either be a slave to sin or to obedience.

When you choose anything other than God to obsess over, you choose sin, even if the thing is not sinful in and of itself.

The obsessed are in danger when their passion draws their gaze away from God, when their hearts are so set on something or someone else that they think they can't live without that thing or person. When this happens, obsession is perverted and used to serve self rather than the God it was meant for, and you find yourself out of control.

Four Categories of Obsession

We obsess over all kinds of different things. A lot of them are ugly, and a lot look really good. Some seem to destroy, while others seem to make you better, so the danger isn't always so obvious. For example, think about what I call **fun obsessions** like romance, love, shopping, talking, getting attention, collecting things, hobbies, happiness, music, friends, family, looking good, and being popular. These all find their birth in the good feelings they give you and seem anything but dangerous. But when those feelings start to grow, you want more of them, and pretty soon in order to get them more often, you need to get what you love more often, which oftentimes leads you to sin in order to get it. That

"Do you not know that if you present yourselves to **anyone** as **obedient** slaves, you are slaves of the one whom you obey.

~ Romans 6:16

thing becomes an obsession, and eventually you can't live without it. This is the beginning of devotion and worship for the obsessed—and the beginning of danger.

Some **destructive obsessions** can come into being this way as well. Things that bring both pleasure and destruction are the more well-known dangerous obsessions, or addictions, as many call them. They are things like drugs, alcohol, cutting, starving, purging, sex, self-condemnation, worry, fear, revenge, gossip, unforgiveness, shame, and guilt. People start out going to these things for relief or refuge, for answers to what bothers them, for hope, for help, for comfort. They take up one of these obsessions because they love what it offers them. And as they continue to go back to it time and time again, they grow in their devotion to it, and soon the obsessed are out of control, a slave to the very thing they thought would set them free.

Another category of obsession is what I call the **frustrating obsessions**. These are annoying habits the obsessed wish they could get away from. Like other types of obsession, these are not something the obsessed bargained for, but although they may be less destructive, they are no less frustrating or hated. Nail biting, scratching, cleaning, obsessive-compulsiveness, being in control, or being perfect are frustrating obsessions that are no less powerful, controlling, or unwanted than drug or alcohol addictions, though perhaps small in comparison.

The final category of obsession is **productive obsessions**. These are less likely to bother the obsessed and might actually be commonly accepted as healthy. If you are obsessed with studying, working, exercising, learning, achieving, being really responsible, eating healthy, or even church activities, you are still obsessed with something other than God. So while these things aren't evil in and of themselves and might actually be productive, they are still competing for your devotion—for your heart, your soul, your strength, and your mind.

It's not that all of these fun, frustrating, or productive obsessions are inherently bad. It's our motives and level of devotion that make them dangerous. When we look to anything other than God to complete us, to protect us, to comfort us, to please us, or to save us, we are looking to another for the very thing God wants to do for us, and we're creating a rival for God's job. That's when being obsessed gets dangerous.

The Source of Obsession

To obsess is to love with your all. When you love someone to the point of obsession, you love them with everything. So to understand your obsession, you have to
understand your love. The most foundational words
on love are found in 1 John 4:19, where we learn that
"we love because he first loved us." These words teach
us the source of love. **True love, authentic love—love
that is selfless, pure, and holy—can only come from
one source: from love himself, God.** So it would stand
to reason that the kind of love you feel for those things
that are inconsistent with his love, those things that
are unholy or that take your gaze off of him, are not
true love. They are only an imitation of true love and a
distraction from it.

True love takes its first step, as Jesus said, in your
all-consuming love for the Father (see Matt. 22:37), but
your love for God isn't something you can generate or
manufacture. It isn't something you must strain to reach
or to guard, but it springs from the beautiful fact that
he first loved you. When you grasp how far and how
deep his love for you goes; when you see the lengths

he went to in order to prove that love to you; when you recognize the beauty of the cross and the necessity of the life of Christ in you, then your love for him is a natural outpouring. When your heart accepts the love of God by accepting his very Spirit into your life, he becomes your obsession.

This book isn't an attempt to condemn your obsessions with the things of this world or to attack your lack of obsession for God. It's to remind you of his love for you so that as you recognize it more and more, your love for him will grow.

So if you are ready to break free from the obsessions that so easily consume you and instead get obsessed with God, let's dive deeper into the life of the obsessed.

2

Obsessed with Loss

I consider everything else worthless because I'm much better off knowing Christ Jesus my Lord. It's because of him that I think of everything as worthless. I threw it all away in order to gain Christ and to have a relationship with him.

Philippians 3:8–9 GW

Stuff becomes our god when we believe that to live without it would be too hard, too dangerous, or too uncomfortable.

Hayley DiMarco

I have obsessed over a lot of things in my life. One of my lifelong obsessions has been disaster. At times I have feared natural disasters so much that if there was any hint of one, I would panic. Tornadoes have sent me straight into the bathtub for protection, sometimes for hours on end, though none were that close. Flying has sent me into a frenzy as in my mind I saw my plane crashing into some sort of brick wall in the sky. Crazy but true. And driving has seemed like such a dangerous thing that I long refused to ride with others because I didn't trust they wouldn't kill us. It used to be that when those I love left the house, a part of me was sure they would never come back because driving was just too dangerous. Yes, I have been obsessed with the fear of disaster. This obsession, though it promised safety, ended up keeping me in a kind of dangerous limbo, because living as if disaster is imminent is living your life in a pseudo disaster. It's exhausting, and it's a waste of strength.

The obsessed are good at focusing. They focus all of their mind and all of their strength on one huge thing. They think about it all of the time, they plan around it, and they are controlled by it. When you are obsessed with loss, well, then you live your entire life expecting loss, which is like living in imaginary loss before you actually lose anything. That means that even though nothing has happened yet, your mindset is such that you are just waiting for the next shoe to drop, so you live each minute as if the loss has already taken place. This kind of thinking paralyzes you. In fact, the one obsessed with loss can feel completely out of control, a victim to the thing that occupies their imagination. A victim of imagined loss.

Those who are obsessed with loss have a problem with fear. When loss becomes a life-altering event, when life is out of control because danger is lurking, at least in your mind, then loss becomes one of the worst things that could ever happen to you. And when you see loss as such a huge and ugly thing, the loss becomes the most important thing in your life, not because you want to think about it more but because you want to avoid it. After all, if you want to avoid it, then you've got to spend time thinking about how, don't you?

Obsessed with Fear and Worry

Fear is something that controls you. **What you fear colors the way you think about life, what you do, what you say, and what you feel.** In the past my fears colored all of my choices and helped decide things like where I would live, what I would do, and who I would marry. Fear is a powerful motivator, and going against your fear seems almost impossible.

Fear promises protection. When you fear something, your body is telling you that danger is ahead and something needs to be done about it. Fear tells you that something bad is about to happen or will happen if you do a certain thing. Most fear comes from the idea that you are going to lose something—your life, your health, your loved ones, your comfort, or your peace. So fear steps into action in order to protect you from potential loss.

When you become obsessed with fear, you are not only controlled by the idea that you have to avoid the thing that you fear but also consumed with the worry that comes along with fear. Fear doesn't just send up cute little red flags for the obsessed to steer around. It pours itself into every part of the life of the obsessed.

So when you become obsessed with fear, you live in a fairly constant state of worry, angst, and dread. Your life is rarely, if ever, calm, rarely at peace for more than a fleeting moment. Fear controls; fear makes demands; fear wants all of your attention. And you give it.

The list of things you can fear, or worry about, is inexhaustible. You can worry about death, pain, running out of money, losing someone you love, being rejected, not being loved, being a victim, or failing. You can fear crowds, small spaces, being trapped, public speaking, spiders, heights, germs, the dark, animals, or flying. Truth be told, we all fear something. Fear is the voice in all of us that warns us that life is too wild, too out of control, too precious to risk being exposed to the thing we fear.

But fear wasn't always a part of our nature as humans. There was a time, when the earth was first made, when fear was nonexistent. Second Timothy 1:7 confirms the truth about fear when it says that "God gave us a spirit not of fear but of power and love and self-control." Fear wasn't present at the beginning, but then something monumental happened: sin entered the world. As soon as it did, Adam and Eve got scared (see Gen. 3:8–10). See, God hung out with them in the Garden on a regular basis, but on the day they ate from the tree of the knowledge of good and evil, they were afraid to see him. **Fear came into the world on the wings of sin.** After the fall, Adam and Eve hid themselves from God. That's exactly what you do when you fear. Rather than coming out into the open with God, you hide from him and from your fears, certain that he has no help to offer, no protection to give. When you obsess over your fear, you remove God from the throne in your life, and your doubt in his goodness and power encourages fear all the more.

To fear anything other than God is to make that thing more powerful than God in your life. Think about it like this: Is what you fear beyond God's ability to protect you? If what you fear is out of his view, reach, or power, then what you fear is more powerful than God, and that means that he is no longer God, because by definition God must be all-powerful and always present. That's part of the nature of God. Your obsession with fear, or worry about the things you fear, declares that God is no longer God but a god with a little *g*—one of many little gods who are unable to manage the entire world, and especially your entire world.

At the time I figured this out, my fear was terrorizing me. I was consumed with all kinds of visions of disaster. There was an accident waiting to happen around every corner. But when I started to consider the attributes of God—his very nature and who he must be in order to be God—a funny thing happened. That fear that used to control me suddenly went silent, or maybe I was deaf to it, but either way, it was shut up. I can remember starting to worry about a big line of tornadoes that was sweeping toward our town, and as we all went down to the basement I thought to myself, *If there is nothing that is out of God's control,* **if everything has to first come through his hands before it gets to me, since he is God, then why would I worry about whatever God decides to give me***, as if his gifts weren't the best thing for me?* As I thought about this my chest began to relax, my blood pressure went back down, and my heart stopped pounding. Believe it or not, I even started to enjoy the sound of the wind and rain. No more begging God to protect us; that's what he does. No more being anxious about nature; that's what he made. No more cowering in fear; that's not faith. When I let this way of thinking permeate my soul, I found that I was no longer obsessed with disaster but became obsessed with a God whose will is perfect and whose ways are pure love. When you can see God in this light, you can be set free from the bondage of obsession.

If you are obsessed with fear or consumed with worry, let my life be a witness to you of the power and sovereignty of God. When you can know that nothing gets past God and that God isn't absent but active in your life, and when you know his power, his ability, his limitlessness, then you have something far better than the fear of man or anything else: you have the fear of God. And unlike all other fears, **the fear of God is good.** Its rewards are great, and so is its power. Just look at what Proverbs has to say about fearing the Lord: "In the fear of the LORD there is strong confidence, and his children will have a place of refuge. The fear of the LORD is a fountain of life to turn one away from the grasp of death" (Prov. 14:26–27 GW). And just for good measure, take a look at Proverbs 19:23: "The fear of the LORD leads to life, and such a person will rest easy without suffering harm" (GW). Did you see all that comes for

To fear anything other than God is to make that thing more powerful than God in your life.

the person who fears the right thing? Confidence, life, safety. In Proverbs 9:10 we learn that "the fear of the LORD is the beginning of wisdom." With that wisdom comes freedom from the fears that used to obsess you. **The fears you have grown to know, the fears that have controlled you, were never meant to obsess you.** In fact, Proverbs 29:25 says, "A person's fear sets a trap for him, but one who trusts the LORD is safe" (GW).

So many obsessed people, so much worry in the world. So much sickness, insomnia, and stress and so many ulcers, phobias, heart problems, digestive problems, and skin problems—all nasty side effects for the wrongly obsessed. When you are obsessed by fear, you imagine all kinds of wrong stuff. You imagine danger and trouble. And in all your imaginings— i.e., worry—you call God a liar. This worry over your safety says that God lied when he told you that you were safe and could have confidence in him. You imagine him a liar when you consider anything else in this world to be more powerful than he is. His Word says, "Almighty LORD, you made heaven and earth by your great strength and powerful arm. Nothing is too hard for you" (Jer. 32:17 GW). When you hear this and yet you imagine that something in your life is too hard for him, you call him a liar.

Those who fear God are blessed (see Ps. 112:1). Sound like the kind of fear you've been experiencing? Or has your fear been more about doubt, danger, death, and the division of your affections? When you fear God more than anything or anyone else, it drives you to confidence in every other area of your life, because what you are more afraid of than anything else is not losing God's love or being left to your own devices but rather that you will not love him in return. When you know the depths of his love and you love him more than anything, even your own life, then you are free to trust him with everything, including your own life. **To fear anything or anyone other than God is to doubt God's sovereignty, love, and power.** It is to say that God isn't sufficient for you, because the things in your life are too much for him to handle or he is too unkind to even care about you and your stuff. But when you fear God, you know that isn't true. You know that he is all-powerful, always present, all-knowing, and all love, and because of that you can be sure that no matter what happens, he is there. No

A person's fear

sets a trap . . . but one who trusts the LORD is safe.

~ *Proverbs 29:25 (GW)*

matter who strikes, he is there. No matter what the pain, he is there, and when he is there, everything is just as it should be.

The key to fear is handing your earthly fears over to the God who loves you. Because he loved you first, you can love him in return. He isn't someone to be scared of. He's not someone to distrust or to doubt but someone to revere, to be in awe of, to love so much that you couldn't dream of disappointing him. When I was little my parents didn't spank me; they didn't need to—not because I was the perfect kid but because I loved them so much that my biggest fear was not pleasing them or not becoming more like them. I did all I could to make my dad proud and to display my love for him. He just had to teach me right from wrong, good from bad, and after that all I wanted was to obey; my love for him compelled me to obedience. The same is true of God as Father: when you stand in awe of him, when you see who he really is, and when you love him for that, you can't help but think of him first. Not returning his love, not submitting to him, and not revering him actually become what you fear more than anything else.

When you love God and when you can accept his love, knowing that it is perfect, not prone to fits of rage, bitterness, or manipulation—that's when you can turn all your fear of everything else over to him and trust him to be sufficient to handle it. His love is the answer to all that you fear. We know this from reading 1 John 4:18, which says, "There is no fear in love, but perfect love casts out fear. For fear has to do with punishment, and whoever fears has not been perfected in love." **God is dead set not on punishing you but on loving you.** He disciplines you, no doubt (see Heb. 12:6), but he will never punish you the way your sins deserve (see Rom. 5:6–8; 8:1) because of his Son.

So don't buy the lie that you can't trust God to save you because your sins are too big. That's a big old lie! If your sins are too big, then Christ died for nothing (see Gal. 2:21). You aren't a special case when it comes to trouble. You aren't a hardship that he just can't manage to save. You aren't unique in your capacity to sin, to fear, or to doubt. We all are equally dense! So don't let the sins of your past color who you think God is, and don't let the things of this world become more important or powerful than God in your life. In the words of the prophet Isaiah, "Don't say that everything these people call a conspiracy is a conspiracy. Don't fear what they fear. Don't let it terrify you" (Isa. 8:12 GW). You have been set free to fear God and God alone. In fact, "You haven't received the spirit of slaves that leads you into fear again. Instead, you have received the spirit of God's adopted children by which we call out, 'Abba! Father!'" (Rom. 8:15 GW). Your Abba, or Daddy, isn't a tyrant, and he hasn't walked out on you, so why do you fear when he is right there with you always? Children fear when they are alone, when their parents aren't there to protect them and care for them, but your Daddy has never left and never will. You can trust him! So change your obsession from the fear of the things of this world to the fear or awe of the God who loves you more than anyone else in the world ever could. Remember that love spends time with the object of its affection. Love is consumed with knowing the loved one more. If you want to stand in awe of God, then make the time in your life to learn why he is so lovable. Devote yourself to knowing him more, and loving him will come naturally.

Obsessed with Doubt

When you are obsessed with losing, you become obsessed with doubt. When what you want, have, or love has become so overwhelmingly important to you that the worst thing in the world that could happen is losing it, your mind can quickly doubt God's provision, protection, or care. You easily obsess over loss because it's the thing you most want to avoid. It's easiest to doubt getting what is the most important to you. When I was younger, food was the most important thing to me. I would get shaky and weak if I didn't eat often enough. If I went for more than a few hours without something substantial, my blood sugar would drop, and I would get light-headed. Food quickly became the most important thing in my life. When I traveled away from home, I would stress over whether there would be suitable food for me. I was so certain I would pass out if I didn't get enough that I doubted continually. In fact, I can remember one retreat with my church group when I ate four or five servings of a meal in an attempt to store up enough food just in case I didn't get to eat the rest of the weekend. I doubted God's provision because I was so obsessed with food.

53

Doubts are bound to pop up in life. Doubting isn't unnatural in the life of faith, but when your doubt of God's protection or provision drives you to take matters into your own hands, you reveal your true obsession. If you doubt that God will bring you a love here on earth and so instead you chase boys, become fixated on finding love, do all you can to make people like you, or give all you can give of yourself for fear of losing your crush, you are obsessed with love. When you doubt God's protection you suddenly find the need to work overtime in order to be safe. To doubt he can or will protect you and instead to become obsessed with your own safety is to be wrongly obsessed.

Isn't it ironic how doubt can so easily become an obsession for the believer? You can doubt God's forgiveness, doubt his presence, doubt his protection, doubt his love. You can doubt he answers prayer, doubt he listens, and doubt he will do anything for you. Yet by definition you are a *believer*, so how has doubt taken over your heart? The thing that faith requires is belief, not doubt. Jesus confirmed this repeatedly as he healed the men and women who came to him in faith. "Jesus turned, and seeing her he said, 'Take heart, daughter; your faith has made you well.' And instantly the woman was made well" (Matt. 9:22). It was her faith that enabled him to heal her. Had she doubted, then according to Jesus, she would not have been healed. Doubt traps you in the very thing you fear. It seals you off from God. In Matthew 13:58 you can see the terrible result of doubting Jesus: "He did not do many mighty works there, because of their unbelief."

When you are obsessed with not having something here on earth, whether it's your life, your loved ones, your looks, your popularity, or your stuff, you doubt God himself. You make the stuff of this earth so important that God takes second place, and not only that but you remove him from the throne of your life. And when you do that, you cannot expect him to answer your prayers (see John 9:31).

If you want to be free from your obsession with loss, then you have to have faith—not in the stuff you might lose but in the God your heart must have. Read the words of James 1:6–8 and see what is required of the believer: "Ask in faith, with no doubting, for the one who doubts is like a wave of the sea that is driven and tossed by the wind. For that person must not suppose that he will receive anything from the Lord; he is a double-minded man, unstable in all his ways."

Obsessed with Justice

When someone hurts you, leaves you, or hates you, forgiving them can feel like a crime, or at the very least a very unsafe thing to do. After all, you reason, if you forgive them, it's like what they did was okay, and that means they might do it again. That's not fair. So in an attempt to control and punish them and to protect yourself, you hold on to forgiveness and guard it with all of your heart so that it never gets out. When you do that, other feelings rush in to deal with the subject—feelings like resentment, bitterness, a desire for revenge, and hatred. All of these sins move into your life and feed your obsession, and it grows and grows, becoming something that colors your whole life.

Justice is something we all inherently believe in. When bad things happen you want someone to pay. Where there is sin, there has to be some kind of justice, and you want to be the one to hand it out. But forgiving takes that opportunity away from you. **When you are** obsessed with unforgiveness, you are obsessed with losing the justice that deep down you are sure must be handed down.

But to that God says this: "Don't take revenge, dear friends. Instead, let God's anger take care of it. After all, Scripture says, 'I alone have the right to take revenge. I will pay back, says the Lord'" (Rom. 12:19 GW). When it comes to justice, trust God to take care of that. Instead, "Put up with each other, and forgive each other if anyone has a complaint. Forgive as the Lord forgave you" (Col. 3:13 GW).

If you obsess over something someone else has done to you, then you are controlled by that event. You are changed by it and ruled by it, and you are not free. But you can be free if you will just stop playing God and start trusting God, and that starts with understanding the nature of your own forgiveness. In Matthew 6:14–15, Jesus puts our forgiveness and others' forgiveness into the same pot and mixes them up. He says, "If you forgive the failures of others, your heavenly Father will also forgive you. But if you don't forgive others, your Father will not forgive your failures" (GW). **You cannot expect forgiveness for your stuff if you can't forgive others**

for their stuff. And forgiveness is essential to the life of faith. Without it you have no access to heaven, so you must allow forgiveness to do its work—not only so that you can be saved in this world from the pains of unforgiveness but also so that you can display the forgiveness God has given you.

Obsessed with Losing Your Guilt

Failure to forgive people who have hurt you isn't the only thing you can become obsessed with. You can also become obsessed with your own guilt. Knowing that all guilt deserves punishment, you can easily decide that your own guilt is too great and you need some serious punishment. In this case, you believe that either God's grace is insufficient for the degree of your sin or he is just unwilling to give it in your particular case. So strong is your sense of justice that you just can't imagine that God could forgive you, and so you live your life with the nagging sense that you have unforgiven sin. This feeling of guilt quickly becomes your obsession.

When people don't feel they can be forgiven by God, they create all kinds of ways to punish themselves. From cutting to starving, from hating to working harder at being good—whatever the punishment, the obsessed is ready to inflict it. This obsession with the loss of justice in the face of forgiveness is life altering and can bring you into all kinds of dark, dark places.

Jesus came to earth with the sole purpose of forgiving sin. It's crucial that you understand that. He gave up everything in heaven in order to come here and suffer. Why? For your forgiveness. So saying that God can never forgive you for what you did, or that you can't accept his forgiveness, is saying God made a huge mistake sending his Son to do a job only you could do. When you are obsessed with guilt, you are obsessed with your own twisted sense of justice.

But there is hope for the obsessed. There is a way out of the pain for the one who needs forgiveness. It's found in taking back your life by way of giving up your life to the God of justice. **The problem for the unforgiven is that they believe their justice is more right, or righteous, than God's,** so they reject his ideas in favor of their own. That's exactly what you do when you fail to accept his forgiveness. Because God is a God of justice

You cannot expect forgiveness for your stuff if you can't

forgive others for their stuff.

he can never be unjust; he is by definition always just. He is also a forgiving God, which means that forgiveness does not contradict justice. In his amazing book *The Knowledge of the Holy*, A. W. Tozer explains God this way: "Between His attributes no contradiction can exist. He need not suspend one to exercise another, for in Him all His attributes are one. All of God does all that God does; He does not divide himself to perform a work, but works in the total unity of His being."[3] So his forgiveness is done in love, in mercy, and in grace, all the while still being just.

Whether you've lied to a friend or loved one, been caught cheating, or said hurtful things about another, convicting guilt is good. But **if you haven't been able to accept God's forgiveness because you demand justice, then you haven't accepted the very nature of God**, who is so forgiving that he would allow his Son to die on a cross in order to save you. Obsess over God and his goodness more than you obsess over your own sense of justice, and you will be set free from the chains that bind you to the past. Jesus came to set you free, not to condemn you. Much is said about John 3:16, and for good reason, but look ahead to the next verse and you'll find these all-important words: "God sent his Son into the world, not to condemn the world, but to save the world" (John 3:17 GW). Stop rewriting history and allowing condemnation to rule your world—Christ came to save you from that very condemnation.

Willing to Lose

If you are obsessed with losing something you find important—your life, your family, your friends, your justice, your popularity, or anything else—then you have lost your God-obsession and your freedom. To be obsessed with anything other than your Lord is to be chained to this world, unable to break free from its tight grip. The apostle Paul is our example when he says, "I consider everything else worthless because I'm much better off knowing Christ Jesus my Lord. It's because of him that I think of everything as worthless. I threw it all away in order to gain Christ and to have a relationship with him" (Phil. 3:8–9 GW). Jesus is so important that Paul "threw it all away." Those are powerful words! To throw it all away is to give up not all your stuff but all your *hope in* that stuff to satisfy and save you. To throw away all that you've worked so hard for—all your popularity, all your happiness, your love, your looks—is to prove you are obsessed in the way you were made to be obsessed. When you can do that, you can be free from debilitating or perceived loss and instead lose yourself to the love of God. Then all that used to obsess you will loosen its grip and fall away, and you will be set free.

3

Obsessed with Gain

Earthly possessions dazzle our eyes and delude us into thinking that they can provide security and freedom from anxiety. Yet all the time they are the very source of anxiety.

Dietrich Bonhoeffer, *The Cost of Discipleship*

Either God is all I need or a supplement is required.

Hayley DiMarco

More is always a good thing, right? Most of us would agree. And most of us want more of what we love. When something is good, it's hard not to want more of it. I definitely know what I'm talking about. If I'm being honest with you, then I have to tell you that I am by nature a glutton. I can't get enough of a good thing. When I make a pie, I eat the entire thing in twenty-four hours. When I see a super cute sweater, I buy it in every color they have. When I get a back rub from my husband, it's a crime for it not to last at least a half hour. I am just not satisfied with a little of a good thing; I want more, more, more! So I call myself a recovering glutton. Fortunately, I know my tendencies and have taken steps to change them because I have seen what my obsession with more can do—land me $20,000 in credit card debt, twenty-five pounds overweight, and heartbroken. Yay, more! (Kidding.)

A lot of our obsessions have to do with getting more of a good thing. Things like love, hobbies, clothes, sleep, romance, and exercise are all so awesome that wanting more and more is an easy thing to do. While those things aren't inherently bad, overdosing on anything is. Obsessing over them can quickly turn a good thing into a really dangerous thing.

How many people throughout history have committed so much of themselves to finding love that their lives have ended in destruction when love couldn't be found? How many people have wanted more stuff so badly that they have put themselves into so much debt that they lost it all? People who are obsessed with gaining more of what they love are in danger of losing exactly what they are after.

Obsessed with Love

Have you ever been obsessed with love? I have. I have had days, even months, when all I could do was think about him, dream about him, and pray about him. I would wake up thinking of him, think about him all day, and then go to sleep thinking about him. I was consumed with the overwhelming feelings of love—so consumed that I could barely do anything else! I had no desire for food, really, and no desire to think about anything else but him. All my conversations were about my love, and everything I did was about impressing him and winning his love. When you are obsessed with love, you are truly obsessed.

Love is an amazing thing. A great gift from a great God. He didn't have to give us the ability to love; he didn't have to give us feelings at all, but he did, and love has to be one of the best of them. But why did he give it to us? Did he give it in order that it might become what we live for? The Bible says "God is love" (1 John 4:8). Does that mean that when you love someone, somehow God is there? Are all the feelings of love that consume you actually God? Of course they aren't, but love is a tricky concept to understand. No one can say anything negative about it, so we all dive into it headfirst as if it's the best thing in the world. Then why does it hurt so much? Why does it feel so great at times yet tear you up at other times? Why is love so hard to come by? And why does it consume you when you finally find it?

Understanding love is one of the most important things you'll ever do, because without a good understanding of it you will be brokenhearted, lonely, and ultimately unable to love anyone other than yourself. So let's dive into love in order to better understand your obsession.

The number one purpose for love is found in Luke 10:27: "Love the Lord your God with all your heart and with all your soul and with all your strength and with all your mind, and your neighbor as yourself." **Love is to be used for God. To love him is your number one goal and the number one purpose for love.** Clearly, without this, true love is not possible. That's why Jesus can follow up his command to love God with everything in you with the command to love others. If loving your neighbor wasn't a part of loving God, then to love God with all or 100 percent of your heart would leave no room for you to love others. Loving your neighbor isn't in addition to loving God (which would require something like 102 percent of your heart) but a *part* of loving God. The purpose of love, according to Jesus, is to love God and your neighbors.

The next big thing we learn about love is found in 1 Corinthians 13, which is the big "love chapter," used at so many weddings. I love this section of Scripture, not because it's so romantic but because it's so honest. Take a look and see what I mean:

Love is patient and kind; love does not envy or boast; it is not arrogant or rude. It does not insist on its own way; it is not irritable or resentful; it does not rejoice at wrongdoing, but rejoices with the truth. Love bears all things, believes all things, hopes all things, endures all things. (1 Cor. 13:4–7)

On the surface this verse might seem really romantic and exciting. After all, who doesn't want to be loved like this? But the thing we have to remember is that this verse isn't about how someone should love *you* but how you should love *others*. That means this verse isn't so much about getting as it is about giving. **When you look closely you can see that it's all about how to behave not around wonderful and exciting people, like cute boys, but around difficult and frustrating people.** After all, some of the things love requires are being patient, not being irritated, not being bossy, not giving up, and not keeping track of all the wrong things people do. Nowhere in this verse does it talk about what love is supposed to do for you; it's all about what you are supposed to do for the one you're loving. And that's the rub. Love isn't about you. That means that love isn't about how you feel. **Certainly it can feel great to be in love, but the great feeling of love was never meant to become an obsession.** It was never meant to be the thing you dream about all day or the thing you wish for with all your heart.

No, love is meant to serve the loved one, not the loving. That's why Jesus also says that we are to love our enemies and to do good to those who hate us (see Matt. 5:44)—because **love isn't about how you feel but about the God you love.** True love's source is God, for God is love, meaning love is a part of his nature and he cannot stop loving. Everything he does is out of love. That means that as his child you will practice love, not because of how it feels to you but because love is who he is and because when you imitate him, it gives him the glory.

Love takes a dangerous turn when it is used to serve self. When you obsess over getting love, being loved, or falling in love, then we are no longer talking about true love but a cheap imitation. **True love involves turning away from pleasing yourself and toward pleasing God.** This might sound harsh and dangerous, but the more you let the Word of God shape your heart and mind, the more it will make sense to you. After all, Jesus was the perfect example of love, and in him we see the ultimate act of selflessness. His journey to the cross was filled not with romance or excitement but with pain and anguish. That didn't make it less loving but more loving. And when he spoke to his disciples, he didn't speak of them taking a different path but told them to take the same one when he said, "If anyone would come after me, let him deny himself and take up his cross and follow me" (Mark 8:34). To follow Jesus means to deny yourself, not serve yourself. Loving God isn't about how you feel but about the gratitude you have for who he is and what he has done.

When love is about you, how it makes you feel, and what it gives you, then it is easy to become wrongly obsessed over it, to do stupid things for it, to compromise your beliefs for it, and even to hurt yourself for it. But when love isn't about you but is about God, who loved us while we were still sinners (see Rom. 5:8), then love is the perfect thing to be obsessed about. **When you are obsessed with loving God, you will automatically love others well and will find all the love you need.** The girl who is obsessed like this can't be destroyed by a broken heart. She can't be devastated by a lack of earthly love. She can't be damaged by rejection, isolation, or even hatred, because her love is secure in the perfect lover, the Father himself.

To be obsessed with God is to find the perfect true love you will never lose again. So many times people are wrongly obsessed with getting more love. What they don't realize is that all the love they could ever need is found in one place and one place alone: in the arms of the Father. From this vantage point, his loving hand is seen everywhere, from the kindness of a friend to even the anger of an enemy. God's love, working in everything he does and doesn't do, in everything he allows to happen in your life or doesn't allow, changes your life for his glory, no matter how bad your circumstances seem. When you know the depths of his love and the reach of his hand, nothing can tear you away from his love—nothing.

If you are obsessed with getting more love, look no further than to the Father. In him there is all the love in the world, and with him your love will be true, it will be eternal, and it will be glorious.

Obsessed with Stuff

I've said it before and I'll probably say it again: there are only two categories of things in this world—God and stuff. So **when you obsess over anything other than God, you are obsessing over stuff**. Stuff isn't all bad; a lot of stuff is essential, like food, water, and clothes. Those are all needs. You've got to have them, so they can't be bad. But when you obsess over them, they go from good for you to bad for you in an instant. That's because when you obsess over stuff you give that stuff the position God was meant to have. You even make it more important than him by thinking about it more and working harder to get it, to keep it, and to use it. When you obsess about stuff, it becomes your little god, and that means God is no longer God to you but an afterthought, a distant memory, a comforting idea—but not a controlling force.

When you obsess over stuff, you treat it with honor and respect. You protect it. You guard it. You worry about it and stress over it because not having it would be the worst thing in the world. When stuff is all-important to you, you collect it, you show it off, or you hide it for

To be
obsessed with God

is to find the

perfect true love

you will never lose again.

fear of losing it. It runs your life. All your plans revolve around the stuff you love; all your hopes and dreams center on getting the stuff you want.

I'm not saying that loving hobbies, sports, clothes, cars, games, or anything else is a bad thing, but when you obsess over anything other than God, that is a terrible thing. God is firm in this position when he says, "You shall have no other gods before me" (Deut. 5:7). You might not consider your passion to be a god, but let me say that it can be. A god is something you serve with all your thoughts, all your strength, and all your soul. A god is something that consumes you and something that guides all your decisions.

For example, think about a girl who is consumed with gymnastics. She has been doing it since she was four, and she is excellent at it. She's so good that she might just make the Olympic team in a few years. But in order to be as good as she is, she has to eat, drink, sleep, and live gymnastics. She has to wake up early to work out. She has to eat right in order to stay strong. She has to go straight to the gym after school. She has to stay till late at night. She has to commit her weekends to it and focus all her thoughts on it. She has to serve it as a god, and because of that, that is exactly what it becomes. When all you have time for is your obsession, when all you talk about is your obsession, when everyone knows you by your obsession—then you have made a god of that obsession.

But the girl who devotes herself to God the Father, who spends early morning hours waking up to talk with him, who can't stop telling others the amazing things he's done, who dreams of doing all she can for his glory, who wants to serve him with all of her life—this girl is obsessed well! It's a good obsession when her life points nowhere but up, when she doesn't divide her worship between him and another, and when everyone who sees her sees him through her. This girl is set free to do and to be whatever he wills for her. She is set free to be just who she was meant to be.

When God gifts you with a talent, it will be all about him. It will serve him, and it will serve you as it grows the gifts of the Spirit in your life. Most importantly, it will not consume you or distract you from God. As we read in 1 Corinthians 6:12, " 'Everything is permissible for me'—but not everything is beneficial. 'Everything is permissible for me'—but I will not be mastered by anything" (NIV 1984). Is excelling in sports permissible?

By all means. Is being a brain surgeon allowable? Certainly. But **if anything you go after masters you; if you are consumed, obsessed, driven by one thing—let it be God himself, and not one of his gifts.** Because remember, there are two things in this world: God and stuff. His gifts, though they are amazing, are stuff, and as good as they may be, they were never meant to consume you and never meant to be your god.

It can be easy to serve the stuff we love, to work hard for it, to set our goals on it, and to strive for it with all our strength, but we have to be aware that serving stuff is a dangerous game to play. God doesn't want you to be ignorant of this propensity to worship stuff, so he says, "You shall not bow down to them or serve them, for I the LORD your God am a jealous God, visiting the iniquity of the fathers on the children to the third and the fourth generation of those who hate me" (Exod. 20:5). These words tell us that God considers our obsessions equal to idolatry—the worship of another god over him. Those are some powerful words, and words that we can't ignore in favor of stuff.

If you have spent any time at all obsessing over stuff, you are not alone. I know of no one who hasn't. Your obsession doesn't disqualify you from faith, though. I've said it before and I'll continue to say it until your heart gets this: it is only "by grace you have been saved through faith. And this is not your own doing; it is the gift of God, not a result of works, so that no one may boast" (Eph. 2:8–9). Allow his grace to enter your life. Accept it and turn away from your old ways; take up his ways and find freedom from the things you obsess over today. You were not meant to obsess over stuff. In it there is no hope for salvation, only effort and strain and heartache. Turn your obsessions upward and be set free! You are no longer a slave to stuff.

Obsessed with Success

No one wants to fail. Failure is uncomfortable, embarrassing, and demeaning. We all work to avoid it and instead strive for success. While success is, humanly speaking, the best result for your efforts, it isn't always the best thing for your soul. The world has convinced us that success is the only good and that failure is not an option. When we fail we want to point the finger to figure out where things went

God considers our obsessions equal to idolatry— the worship of another god over him.

wrong. We start to make accusations against ourselves and even against our God. But failure isn't always a bad thing. To the world that looked on, Jesus was the ultimate failure. He was supposed to rescue the Jews, to lead an army, to make a difference, but all he did was die on a cross, naked and alone. Yet his "failure" was your salvation! His death made way for his resurrection, and his resurrection made possible the salvation of all of mankind.

For centuries people have failed and God has won. God can have victory even in loss, but still we all prefer gain. So we focus on finding success and being the best, the most popular, the most loved, the most famous. We are so convinced that success is the only acceptable outcome that we do all we can to avoid its opposite.

But when you obsess over success, you set yourself up for failure, because though you might achieve your goals, you fail at the most important things in life. You miss out on things like trust, hope, perseverance, and patience. These are things that you learn through failure, through difficulty, and through trial. Worldly success teaches the soul very little. In fact, some of the most successful people in the world are also the most emotionally and spiritually tortured people. **Success isn't a training ground for spiritual growth, but suffering and trials are.** That is why some of the most interesting people in the world aren't the rich and famous but those who have been through great trials and difficulties. This is what shapes you and makes you into the likeness of Christ, who "although he was a son . . . learned obedience through what he suffered" (Heb. 5:8). God has a different economy than the rest of the world. He values what the world fears. He cherishes what it wants to avoid. In James 1, you are told that you are to consider it pure joy "when you meet trials of various kinds, for you know that the testing of your faith produces steadfastness. And let steadfastness have its full effect, that you may be perfect and complete, lacking in nothing" (vv. 2–4). In God's economy it isn't success that makes you perfect and complete. It isn't success that makes you successful but something altogether different. **When you define success as nothing but loving God with all your heart, soul, mind, and strength, then you are successful no matter what might happen.**

Obsessed

While you might believe that being popular, famous, or successful is the best thing for you, God might be thinking something different. He might have more than that in store for you. He might want to bless you with weakness (see 2 Cor. 12:9), with suffering (see Matt. 5:4), or with poverty (see Luke 6:20). He might want to push you to your physical limits so that there will be nothing left of you and all that's left will be of him. He might want you to prove his faithfulness in your failure, in your anonymity, or in your suffering. All I know is that with less of you, there is more of him. In the words of John the Baptist, "He must increase, but I must decrease" (John 3:30). Success always has you as its root. It's all about how you look, how you feel, and what you do. That's why it can easily become an obsession: because you are so high on you that you want to have all that you want and be all that you can be. Again, this is not a shot in the dark for me to say, because it's true of every one of us. We are all about ourselves; it's our human nature. Deep down we all crave success of some kind.

Obsessing about success sets you up for heartache, because success isn't always possible. When you can't reach or keep the object of your obsession, your entire body, mind, and spirit can be thrown out of whack. In that process you can find yourself in more pain, in more distress, and in more agitation than you ever imagined. When you obsess over something other than God, it will eventually disappoint you, and when it does, you have nowhere to turn. But when you obsess over God, devoting yourself to serving him and knowing him, then success or failure is simply the next step that he has for you to take. It is irrelevant in the grand scheme of things, except that it is from his hand. I'm not saying that your goal should be failure—that would just be a new obsession—but your goal as a follower of Christ is meant to be him and him alone. Since he never fails, you will never find failure to be a problem in your life. When you obsess over God everything spent on him is success.

Obsessed with Self

When you define success as serving and pleasing God rather than yourself, you have defined success well, and you are more certain to find success than when you define it as serving self. Your "self" is a dangerous master who isn't easily satisfied. The eye never gets enough of

When you obsess over God, devoting yourself

to serving him
and knowing him,
then success or failure is
simply the next step that
he has for you to take.

seeing, the senses never get enough of sensing. Self is never satisfied when its goal is self-serving. But how easy it is to obsess over self! After all, you are with yourself 24 hours a day. You have to care for yourself, feed yourself, and protect yourself, so of course self is often at the forefront of your mind. But when you are consumed with yourself, then you're in trouble, because self will ultimately destroy itself.

I know what I'm talking about. For most of my life I have been obsessed with self. I have pampered myself, comforted myself, and served myself with honor and respect. When my self wanted something, I rushed to get it. When my self was bored, I fed it. When it was tired, I let it sleep and sleep and sleep. I can remember those days when I believed I needed twelve hours of sleep a day. So that's what I did—I slept twelve hours, then got up and went to work. On my lunch hour I would come home and take a nap—a nap!—so much did my self love sleep.

Gluttony of any kind is simply proving that you are obsessed with yourself. If you are a glutton for exercise or for soap operas, for gossip or for patriotism, you are simply showing your obsession with self. Indulging in something to an extreme serves self. **If there is anything you just can't get enough of, that's a real red flag for obsession with self.** While self does have needs that have to be fulfilled, you have to realize that the only things self *really* needs are food, water, air, shelter, clothing, community, and God. If you use the word *need* a lot, stop and consider if what you are talking about fits one of those categories. Is it a real need, or is your self doing all the talking?

I find that serving my self is slavery of the worst kind, because I am never satisfied, and I let myself know that. Then discontentment, complaint, grief, resentment, bitterness, stress, and a whole lot of other ugly emotions seep out of my heart and my mouth and pollute my whole life. With self as our god, we are destined for any number of heartaches like depression, guilt, anger, worry, and fear. When the god you serve is incapable of controlling the world around you, of managing your emotions, and of doing things that can only be done by God, eventually your obsession is going to emotionally damage you.

But you don't have to be obsessed by your self. You can turn it over to the One who is worthy of obsession. You can give up living for your self and live for him. You can change your way of life and your way of thinking simply by stopping the insanity of self-worship. As you realize that you aren't perfect, that there is no one who is (see Rom. 3:10), that you can't control anyone or anything around you, and that you are a sinner (see Rom. 3:10–11), you see that your only hope of salvation is Jesus Christ (see Acts 4:12). When you realize that you aren't worthy of his love but he loves you anyway—that in fact he loves you no matter what you've done or are going to do and will never leave you or forsake you (see Heb. 13:5)—you begin to fully turn your worship over to God himself and find yourself set free from the pains and turmoil associated with serving self. Then you will be able to say with Paul, "For to me to live is Christ, and to die is gain" (Phil. 1:21). When you live for Christ, all is good—even what others consider bad—because everything has the fingerprints of God on it (see Lam. 3:37–38; Matt. 28:18; John 3:27).

Obsessions threaten to destroy lives by the millions, but believers obsessed with God have changed this world and continue to change it for the better. Lives that are turned over not to God but to his creation (see Rom. 1:25) are on a trajectory of destruction if they don't put away their obsessions and exchange them for the only obsession that truly saves.

When the human soul, designed to obsess over God, turns and obsesses over something or someone else, it suffers. Obsession of any kind other than obsession with God consumes the soul that is devoted to it, saps its strength, and occupies the mind. Those obsessed with perfection are eaten up by their imperfection, and those obsessed with their bodies are grieved by its continual decay. When people obsess over the finite instead of the infinite they cheat themselves of the very thing God wants to give them: salvation from the sin that so easily consumes them. And that's ultimately why we obsess: we obsess in order to gain what we discern is freedom—freedom from pain and suffering, from rejection, or from danger. But the only real freedom we can have is living our lives fully for Christ, accepting his atonement for our sins, accepting his complete work, and letting go of our own efforts to save ourselves.

4

Obsessed with Relief

The prime purpose for seeking help ought not to be relief from some difficulty, but ought to be to please the Lord whether or not relief comes.

Jay Adams

When you determine that suffering is not your end but your beginning, you are set free and the enemy loses.

Hayley DiMarco

When I was young I had really bad cramps. Oh, the pain! Every month the agony was almost more than I could bear. I don't deal well with pain; it's not something I welcome or even tolerate, so when the pain got to be so bad that I screamed and keeled over on the floor of the bathroom, I decided that maybe hitting my head on the porcelain sink would overwhelm my cramps and give me some relief. I banged and banged in order to dull the pain in my gut with a sharper pain on my head. Sounds crazy, I know, but pain can make you do some crazy things. In fact, trying to avoid pain is probably one of the most common actions in the world. No one wants to suffer, not even those of us who inflict it on ourselves. We are all just trying to dull one pain with another.

When I talk with my friends, the most common conversations are ones about relief. We want relief from heartache, loneliness, physical pain, doubts, fears, guilt, and even God. We suffer in our bodies and in our souls and we want it to stop, so we talk and talk about our suffering and about the things that relieve it. We complain, we question, we search for relief, wanting life to be less about what hurts and more about what helps.

It's about the age-old questions: Why me? Why this? Why now? Why do I suffer so much, and more importantly, how do I stop it? These questions are so urgent that we continue to ask them day in and day out. We plead with God about them, we look for answers, and we try whatever medication promises the quickest relief from our pain. Before you know it, we are obsessed not with God but with relief from what hurts inside of us.

The problem is that the pain of suffering can be so loud, so controlling, so angry that nothing else can be heard over its cry, and we can't think about anything else. While suffering lingers, so does the obsession over it. This leads us to try applying medication in order to lessen and control the pain. When you think of medication you may think of prescription drugs, but that's not the only kind of medication there is. Medication can come in the form of anything that distracts you from whatever you are feeling that you don't like. **Medication is just another word for relief.** When the discomfort in your life is more than you can bear, relief becomes your number one goal in life—the thing you think about more than anything else, talk about more than anything else, and want more than anything else. When that happens, you are obsessed.

Obsessed with Comfort

Most people believe that Satan's goal is to make you suffer, to torture you and hurt you, and to bring pain into your life, but **Satan is served well when you search for comfort through obsession.** He doesn't need to make you suffer; he can make just as much progress when you are comfortable. In fact, he may even make more progress when everything is great because often in those moments you see no need for God.

When you are medicated by comfort, the pain meant to drive you to your knees is eased. The pain that would purify you and teach you perseverance and wisdom is silenced, and the joy that should come from being drawn to your Savior's side is gone.

You can see the danger of being obsessed with comfort when you look at addictions. Look at the reasons behind them—comfort, relief, escape—and then look at the destruction they bring. An addiction is simply misplaced worship. It is a spiritual problem that can quickly turn into a physical one. When you need comfort, you have two places to turn: to the world and all it offers, or to the Father and all he is. If you turn to the world, you turn your back on the saving power of the Father, and instead you pick up the destructive power of the world. Thus begins your addiction to, or obsession with, comfort and happiness in whatever form they come.

That means that when pain and suffering come, the comfort-obsessed immediately freak out, because pain is inconsistent with happiness, and they go into medication mode. They look around frantically for something, anything, that can numb the pain, cover it up, or take it away. In some cases they take drugs; in others they look for another feeling like love to fix it. Whatever it might be, when you look for relief anywhere other than in the arms of the Father, you aren't healing the source of the pain but multiplying the pain by becoming wrongly obsessed over something that was never meant to be your comfort, never meant to be your source of joy.

When comfort is king, it can be very easy to start to obsess over it, and suddenly nothing else but comfort will do. You know you have a problem with comfort when it's the first thing you think about when making a choice about what to say or what to do. I have been obsessed with comfort most of my life, and looking back, I can see countless times when I chose my own comfort over kindness, joy, and even love. I have been so attached to comfort that I have done rude things, unthinkable things to other people and even to myself. I've bought things I couldn't afford and gone into debt for it. I've rejected people, ignored people, and judged people who made me uncomfortable. I've ignored God, looked to the world, grown lazy, turned to food, become self-absorbed—all because of my obsession with comfort.

Comfort comes in many forms. In fact, we all adore comfort in some way or another. **To find out if you obsess over comfort, just look at where you go for relief.** What do you turn to when you have had a terrible day? Where do you go when life gets hard? What do you have to have in order to be happy? What do you tell yourself you must have, period? The answers to these questions help you discover your comfort obsession. Comfort, or relief from the pains of life, points to your god. Have you made comfort king of your life? If you have, then you are obsessed with comfort.

Comfort is a passion for pain avoidance. Any pain or discomfort, as some would call it, makes you crazy and must end as soon as possible. In the mind of the comfort-obsessed, pain is evil and comfort is great. So you are always on the lookout for pain, and at the first sight of it you either run or medicate, because you can't see any purpose in it. **But pain was meant to serve a spiritual purpose**, as we can see in Romans 5:3–5:

> We know that suffering creates endurance, endurance creates character, and character creates confidence. We're not ashamed to have this confidence, because God's love has been poured into our hearts by the Holy Spirit, who has been given to us. (GW)

Pain and the suffering it produces have a big spiritual payoff: endurance. Endurance comes from making it through something, not medicating it, not fearing it, and not arranging your life to completely avoid it. I'm not talking about enduring suffering and pain in the sense of going into surgery without anesthesia or anything. But when you endure the suffering and pain of being uncomfortable, you strengthen your endurance and character, and the end result is the confidence that comes from having a heart filled with God's love.

Obsessed with Pain

While many of us are always on the lookout for comfort, some just remain obsessed with the pain. If you talk about your pain all the time; if people know you by your pain; if it's the subject of all your Facebook status updates, all your blog posts, and all your conversations, then you are obsessed.

Some people let their physical pain and suffering define them, but you were never meant to be defined by your suffering. Instead Christ's suffering should be your focus, because it was through his suffering that you were saved, not your own. **But when you rehearse your pain, when you make it the star of your life, then his sufferings take the back seat, and yours then becomes your hope for salvation.** As you obsess over your pain, your worship gets misplaced and your obsession for the Father becomes a fading memory.

To find out if you

obsess over comfort,

just look at where you go for relief.

Obsessed with Wounds

If you are old enough to be reading this, then you are old enough to have been hurt. We have all been hurt; it's just part of living on this earth. Much of that hurt has gone unhealed, unattended to, and uncleansed, and when that happens, hurts turn into wounds. Wounds are those gaping holes in your life where something happened that changed you. Something someone did to you, either intentionally or accidentally, altered your life forever, and because of that a wound was opened and never closed back up.

When you get a cut on your skin and you put a Band-Aid on it, over time that skin scabs over. Soon the scab falls off and the wound is gone, replaced by fresh new skin. But if you were to keep picking the scab, ripping it off, and not giving it time to do its job, you wouldn't allow your skin to heal. The same is true of your emotional wounds. When you keep coming back to them and opening them up; when you worry over them, ponder them, and resent them, you are picking at the scab and deepening your wound. **But wounds weren't meant to be permanent; your body and your soul were meant to**

106

be healed. When you reject healing and instead major in woundedness, you become obsessed with your wounds instead of Christ's wounds. **The only wounds that really matter in this world are the wounds Jesus received on the cross.** Those are the only ones that were meant to bring healing, the only ones worth thinking about because of their great value. His wounds, not yours, deserve all of the attention. When you can focus on him, remembering his wounds on the cross and all the pain that came with them, you can be sure of your healing. The relief that you so long for will be yours with no ugly side effects.

It can be easy to become preoccupied with your pain, focusing on it and allowing it to define you, but it was never meant to do that. No, your pain was meant to make you stronger, not to oc-cupy all your thoughts. **Pain makes you stronger when you let it do its work and then let it pass, not becoming addicted to it by reliving it or in-flicting it upon yourself.**

The only wounds that really matter in this world are the wounds Jesus received on the cross.

Obsessed with Emotional Pain

Sometimes feelings can hurt just as bad as physical pain. Bad feelings can come at you from all kinds of places: from past memories, from current relationships, from circumstances within your control and circumstances beyond your control. And when those feelings come, they can overrun your entire life. When that happens, the first thing you want to do is find a way out, and as long as you remain more obsessed with how you feel than with God, the way out will ultimately be the way right back into pain.

It works like this: When you are obsessed with relieving your emotional pain, when it consumes you and you can't go on any longer, you look for a quick fix or a replacement emotion. You pick up a drink, a cigarette, a razor blade, or a doughnut, and you embrace the feeling that thing gives you in order to mask your uncomfortable emotion. This artificial emotion then soothes your pain, medicating it, treating the symptom of discomfort rather than the cause. As with all medication for symptoms, the comfort soon wears off, and you either need more medication or you're stuck right back in the middle of the pain you thought you had left. Of course you want relief, so you medicate some more. Before you know it, your bad feelings are no longer your obsession, but the medication is. You tell yourself you have to have it. At this point you have become obsessed with making yourself feel a certain way.

All kinds of addictions, afflictions, and problems come from trying to ease the sting of bad feelings. But the problem with emotional pain is that it demands an obsession to take its place. You can't get rid of persistent emotional pain without replacing it with something greater, stronger, and more consuming. You can try things like eating more, eating less, cutting, drinking, or drugs to ease your emotional turmoil, but these things are insufficient to remove the cause of the pain. They are a Band-Aid, a cover-up, and they are ineffective. All they tend to do is to send you into a different kind of emotional turmoil, adding layer upon layer to your suffering.

When you are obsessed over your emotional pain, controlled by it and consumed with it, and you look to another earthly obsession to comfort you, you never succeed because you misunderstand the power of feelings. The person who is obsessed with God gives little power to painful feelings, because bad feelings have a simple remedy: truth. **Truth heals emotional pain better than any other medicine you can apply.** Truth heals emotional pain because truth resets your heart and your mind and calibrates your emotional life to the life of Christ. And that life of Christ sets you free (see John 8:32). It sets you free from the wages of sin and its powerful grip. When that happens, emotional pain loses its power.

The truth that must be grasped by everyone who wants to obsess over God rather than their feelings is the truth of who God is. Do you know that **God is all-powerful, all-knowing, and always present**? Do you know that **he knows everything there is to know about you, and he loves you anyway**? Do you know that **he is kind and gentle, wise and good**? Do you know that **he is sovereign**? That means that he's not just watching your life from a distance but he's actively involved, touching every aspect of your life here on earth. Not too impressed with the job he's doing? That's only because you don't trust him. When you look at the world with earthly eyes, all can seem lost, but from God's heavenly perspective, all is well.

Just look at the life of Joseph (see Gen. 37–50). He was sold by his brothers into slavery and later put into prison. So many horrible things happened in his life, but they had to happen to get him where he had to go. The same is true for all believers who trust God: nothing that happens to you is in vain. Nothing is pointless or senseless, but all is meant to drive you deeper into obsession with God. All is meant to serve as a catalyst to get you to his feet. And all will do its work when you can see his hand in everything and trust that he works it all out for the good of those who love him (see Rom. 8:28).

Emotional pain may come to us all, but it can be gone almost as quickly as it comes if you consider who it came from. One of my favorite authors is Charles Spurgeon. He wrote long, long ago these incredibly uplifting words that I think apply perfectly to this discussion: "It would be a very sharp and trying experience to me to think that I have an affliction which God never sent me, that the bitter cup was never filled by his hand, that my trials were never measured out by him, nor sent to me by his arrangement of their weight and quantity."[4]

Truth heals emotional pain

better than any other

medicine you can apply.

Spurgeon suffered from the emotional pain of depression. He suffered a lot, but he never became obsessed with his pain because he believed in its holy purpose. In fact, he once said, "I am afraid that all the grace that I have got of my comfortable and easy times and happy hours, might almost lie on a penny. But the good that I have received from my sorrows, and pains, and griefs, is altogether incalculable. . . . Affliction is the best bit of furniture in my house. It is the best book in a minister's library."[5]

When you give credit for your pain to anyone or anything other than God, you are a victim, but when you can faithfully accept it as coming from him, you are blessed. My favorite verse when it comes to emotional grief and suffering is found in Lamentations 3:37–38: "Who has spoken and it came to pass, unless the Lord has commanded it? Is it not from the mouth of the Most High that good and bad come?" The truth is that "A person cannot receive even one thing unless it is given him from heaven" (John 3:27), so why would we obsess in agony over our situation when every moment in life is a gift from the most perfect being, love himself, who has no equal in wisdom, faithfulness, grace, or strength?

When you consider the amazing character of God, his unchangeable nature, his reliability, and his goodness, you cannot give your emotional pain one more minute of attention, but you must turn all of your heart, soul, mind, and strength toward him. When you do, and you can see that he has allowed it all, you will be set free from all of the emotional suffering you have been feeling, and you will be rightly obsessed.

Finding relief from the hard parts of life isn't a bad thing. It's something that God wants to give each of us. But when finding relief becomes so important that it clouds our vision of God, then we are obsessed. You may have a lot of suffering in your life and you may have found ways to ease the pain and stay comfortable, but if those things you've gone to for relief now control you, then today is the day to let them go. You can trust God to be all you need when the pain hits. You can trust him to work all things together for your good. But you must trust him. You can't hedge your bets by having a backup plan for the pain. God must be all. He must be your comfort, your happiness, and your rock.

When you can find God's hand by looking into his Word and seeing that he never leaves you (see Heb. 13:5), that he is perfect and that his ways are far above your ways (see Isa. 55:8–9), and that what looks like tragedy from your point of view is progress from his (see Rom. 8:28), then you can be set free from your obsession with finding relief. Pain becomes a distant memory for the girl who looks at life from God's perspective rather than her own. When she trusts his love, his wisdom, and his hand in her life, nothing is life-threatening because her life is hidden in his, and there is perfect peace. Relief is a good thing, and you can thank God when it comes, but don't let the search for relief become more important than your God.

5

Obsessed with God

My goal is God Himself, not joy, nor peace,
Nor even blessing, but Himself, my God;
'Tis His to lead me there—not mine, but His—
At any cost, dear Lord, by any road.

Frances Brook, "My Goal Is God Himself"

You have formed us for Yourself, and our hearts
are restless till they find rest in You.

Augustine

The obsessed are consumed by the object of their affections. They become defined by the very thing they obsess over. The one who obsesses over athletics is an athlete; the one who obsesses over food is a foodie; the one who obsesses over cleanliness is a neat freak; and the girl who obsesses over God is a God Girl. You are defined by the devotion of your heart, the focus of your thoughts, and the use of your energy.

It would follow, then, that if you identify yourself as a Christian, your "soul" obsession is meant to be God himself, because your obsession points to the object of your devotion. If he is your Savior and your first love, he is meant to be your only obsession. You cannot focus your heart, soul, mind, and strength on two different things, so if God isn't your obsession, he isn't your only god.

The obsessed find extreme joy in the object of their obsession. When I look at people who are crazy excited—screaming and jumping up and down about something, anything—I know exactly what they are obsessed with. The obsessed glory in the object of their obsession. This glory, or extreme happiness or elation, is wrapped up in the obsessed getting just what they wanted and bragging about and giving praise to the thing that gave it to them, whether it's the victory, the pleasure, or the success.

This isn't a surprise since we were all made with one express purpose: to give glory to God. We're built to shout from the rooftops, to jump for joy, to rejoice. But was the glory we were made to give meant to be shared? To be spread around to other obsessions? Perhaps not, since 1 Corinthians 10:31 tells us, "Whether you eat or drink, or whatever you do, do all to the glory of God." *All* is an inclusive word; it doesn't mean "part," "some of," or "most of" but "everything." Do it *all* to the glory of God.

But, you say, can't some of my glory be shared? Can't I give glory to other things, good things, that God has allowed in my life as gifts from him? While that sounds right and good, to glory in anything other than God himself is to divide your adoration, your heart, your soul, and your mind. And while you may appear to be faithful for a while, eventually, when a choice must be made between your two obsessions, God's glory will be set up against the other obsession's glory, and a rivalry will be born. Unfortunately for the obsessed, "the LORD is a God who does not tolerate rivals. In fact, he is known for not tolerating rivals" (Exod. 34:14 GW).

That leaves the obsessed with two choices: to be obsessed with God or with his rivals. The God-obsessed are those who find the strength to reject all other competitors for the glory due their God and instead pursue a life bent on loving the Lord their God with all their heart, soul, mind, and strength. This kind of single-minded pursuit destroys all other obsessions and releases you from their brutal grip. **If you want freedom from obsession, then obsess over God from this day forward.**

The God-Obsessed

The first thing you find when you are God-obsessed is that you want God's glory over everything else. You want it more than success, happiness, dreams, or relationships. When the glory of God starts to find competition in anything or anyone else, the God-obsessed prefer him over everything else. If anything gets in the way of bringing glory to God, they will go around it or trample over it. They reject everything that would chain them to this earth—that would keep them here if given the choice between living here with their stuff or being in heaven with the Father. **When given the choice, the God-obsessed always choose God over everything and everyone else.**

To the outsider this can look like a hard thing. To reject the things and even the people you love in favor of God just sounds wrong to many. That's why a lot of people are so uncomfortable with these words of Jesus: "Whoever loves father or mother more than me is not worthy of me, and whoever loves son or daughter more than me is not worthy of me" (Matt. 10:37). God wants us to love our families, but why would he tell us we can't love them as much as we love him? Because of obsession. When you love someone as much as God, your heart is divided, as you put the same value on that person as you were meant to put on God. When you do this it becomes very hard in times of testing to choose God over a loved one. And when another person means as much to you as God, then your tendency is to obsess

over them, giving them equal glory as you give God—
and sometimes even more.

But the God-obsessed can quickly choose God over
everything and everyone else. Nothing stands in the
way of worship. Nothing becomes more important
than giving him the glory—not love, not affection, not
happiness. Nothing brings the joy, thankfulness, or
adoration that God brings to the God-obsessed. There
is great freedom and peace in this state of obsession,
because when you obsess over God like this, circumstances no longer play games with your emotions because all of your hope, joy, and peace are wrapped up
in the unshakable, perfect love of God. He who will
never leave you or give up on you, who is always with
you, always powerful, and always wise cannot be lost.
He cannot be ripped from your life, he cannot aban-
don you, and he cannot disappoint you. **When you are
God-obsessed, you are free from the emotional
turmoil of finding your happiness in the
stuff of this world.** When you are God-
obsessed, you always choose God over all
other pleasures and passions of this earth
because he is your highest pleasure.

Second, **when you are obsessed with God, you want his will to be done. That means that you are content with his will, even if it contradicts your own.** In other words, you are content to be the loser so that God can be the winner. When this is your attitude, nothing that happens to you is too bitter because you are set on his glory and not your own, and when his glory is found even as you suffer, your joy is complete and nothing can hurt you. To be obsessed this way is to find that you are free. No chain can hold you down and nothing in the world can harness you, control you, or use you. The God-obsessed are able, as Paul was, to be content in any and every situation because they want nothing more than God's will (see Phil. 4:11), and they are convinced that in a life bent on glorifying God, nothing less than God's will can ever come to pass.

Finally, **when you are obsessed with God, you will find yourself totally content to be last, to be outdone by others, to be rejected, and to be the least so that he can be the most.** The God-obsessed are no longer self-obsessed but have transferred all of their attention and passion onto the Most High. Because of that they have no need to shine, no need to receive any glory at all, but are happy to live in humility and meekness. This humility, the same kind we see in the life of Christ, isn't an ugly thing that means you are too shy to speak or too insecure to act. It is the strength of spirit that says, "I am nothing so that he may be everything!" (see John 3:30). This humility that removes self from the throne so that God may be put there is a strength of spirit that allows you to be content in any and every situation. It is what allows you to find joy in the suffering, as we see in James 1. It is what allows you to be free from the chains of bondage to this world, the chains that promise you freedom, happiness, and success but only bind you tighter to sin and suffering. When you are obsessed with God, you are certain that the last will be first and that God will lift up the humble and knock down the proud (see Matt. 20:16; 1 Pet. 5:6). The God-obsessed cannot be destroyed by the actions of people because they see in everything the chance to bring glory to God, and that is their chief end. As long as they can do that, they are free. No matter what chains the world may threaten to bind them with, they will always be free.

The God-obsessed are the most joyful and content people on the planet, because nothing can separate

When you are obsessed with God, you want his will to be done. That means that you are content with his will even if it contradicts your own.

them from their Savior; nothing can alter his plans or change his course. But a lot of people who call themselves Christians are less than obsessed with God. Many are slaves to something other than God and suffer from addiction, from emotional pain, from doubt, from fear and worry. If you count yourself as one of those, have no fear—God can change your obsession and give you back your life from the things that control you. It all starts with your thoughts about him. God empowers you to obsess over him as he gives your heart the desire to make bringing him glory your sole purpose in life. When he does that, nothing can stop you. As you look at the lives of those who have heard the call of obsession, you will see a few similar things. They all believe, confess, bear fruit, are content, live consecrated lives, study, praise, and continually tell others about their amazing obsession. Let's take a look at these common traits found in the God-obsessed.

Faith

All obsession starts with faith: a belief that you need the object of your obsession. This is true for the

God-obsessed. In order to love God, to want him and to need him, you must first have faith in him. In Hebrews 11:6 we read that "whoever would draw near to God must believe that he exists and that he rewards those who seek him."

In Romans 4:20–21 we see how giving glory to God grows a strong faith when we read this about Abraham: "No unbelief made him waver concerning the promise of God, but *he grew strong in his faith as he gave glory to God*, fully convinced that God was able to do what he had promised." Abraham's faith was rock solid in believing God's promises were true, and your faith brings glory to God because it proves that you believe he is true (see John 3:33). Without faith you can't consent that God can be trusted and that his words are true. But God honors your faith because your faith honors and brings glory to him. Your faith in God says that there are no impossibilities with God and that he can be trusted with your life, even with your sufferings. When you obsess over God, pointing everything in your life to him, including your ups and your downs, and you want nothing more than to love and serve him, then you are set free from the chains of this world as you are lifted up into the heavenly arms of the Father. And nothing can make you waver because you know that "our God whom we serve is able to deliver us" (Dan. 3:17).

This kind of faith brings glory to God as it announces to the world that he is trustworthy and that nothing can disprove his Word, his promises, and his presence.

Confession

The fastest way to become obsessed with the things of this earth is to fail to admit to God and even to yourself that giving those things more glory than God is sinful. Confessing this sin sets you free from your obsession as you admit that he was right and you were wrong. You also affirm that he is holy and deserves all your affection and devotion and that you have been serving yourself and not your God. In 1 John 1:9 we read, "If we confess our sins, he is faithful and just to forgive us our sins and to cleanse us from all unrighteousness." This is the way God begins to restore your life and free you from obsession. He compels you to confess your obsession, to agree with him that you have sinned, and then he offers you forgiveness that heals you and makes you whole again.

If you are having trouble believing that God can forgive you, it might be time to find a godly person you can trust and confess to them. James 5:16 says there will be healing when you admit your sin to others. It says that you should "confess your sins to one another and pray for one another, that you may be healed. The prayer of a righteous person has great power as it is working." **Don't let the fear of punishment keep you from the grace of forgiveness.** Be brave and admit your obsession. Admit your misplaced worship and begin the process of breaking free.

When you realize the depth of God's love for you and the complete forgiveness that he offers, not based on who you are or your goodness but on his Son's, you no longer fear his punishment or wrath but are free to rest in his grace. This idea is beautifully spelled out in 1 John 4:18–19, which says, "There is no fear in love, but perfect love casts out fear. For fear has to do with punishment, and whoever fears has not been perfected in love. We love because he first loved us." Recognizing his love for you leads you to love him, and this love casts out the fear of punishment that you expected. Your love for him drives you to confession and prepares you for forgiveness, and then it sets you free from obsessing over the things of this world.

Fruit

The fruit of your life points to your obsession. The areas where you shine and where you focus your efforts, spend your energy, and grow the most point to the passion of your heart. Wherever you obsess will be where you grow your fruit. If you obsess over anything other than God, the fruit of your life will be not the fruit of the Spirit but the fruit of the flesh. The girl who obsesses over her body may grow the fruit of worry, fear, and angst in her life. She may grow the fruit of beauty and self-obsession, but she doesn't grow the fruit of the Spirit.

A tree is known by its fruit (see Luke 6:44). Whatever a tree grows the most defines it. When you grow the fruit of the Spirit, you prove the power of God in a life obsessed with him. The fruit of the Spirit isn't something that you must work at, because it is a product of the life of God in you, but it is something that you must be mindful of. You must want it in your life before God will begin the work of it. But when you start to see God's commands regarding the fruit and his desire for you to have an abundance of it in your life (see Gal. 5:22–23), you will start to look for opportunities to walk away from the fruit of the flesh and begin to obsess over God. When you believe the words of Jesus, "By this my Father is glorified, that you bear much fruit and so prove to be my disciples" (John 15:8), your obsession for his fruit begins to grow. And when you define your life by the Spirit rather than the flesh, you give God the glory. As we read in Matthew 5:16, you should "let your light shine before others, so that they may see your good works and give glory to your Father who is in heaven." The fruit in your life—including the godly reactions of your heart and mind to the trials of this life, like difficult people and difficult situations—brings glory to God. As you become obsessed with God, you become obsessed with the fruit of his Spirit.

The fruit of the Spirit is

love, joy, peace, patience, kindness, goodness, faithfulness, gentleness, self-control.

~ Galatians 5:22–23

Contentment

Contentment says, "God has put me in this condition. He could have saved me from it. He could have lifted me out of this mess, but he thought it best to allow this in my life. My life is God's to direct (see Prov. 16:9). If he thinks this is the best for me, then maybe what I would have preferred would have been dangerous for my soul. So I will be content with my situation." When you think like this, you give great glory to God and you prove your obsession is not for yourself but for him. The secret to this contentment is not your hard work but the devotion brought on by your love for him. When you love God because you know that God is good, sovereign, kind, just, and faithful; when you trust him with everything in your life; and when you reject the things of this world that promise to protect you from his wrath, then you find contentment in any and every situation.

Contentment begins with gratitude. You must first be thankful for your life, including even your struggles, as an extension of the very hand of God (see Jer. 18:6), guiding you and keeping you. After you give thanks, you must refuse to make any complaint (see Phil. 2:14).

Complaining accuses God of being less than good. It proves your self-obsession, not your God-obsession. But your contentment glorifies God as it says to all that he can be trusted. Even if the earth gives way, he is still God and still good (see Ps. 46:2).

Consecration

To consecrate something is to set it apart for one purpose. When you obsess over God, his glory is your one purpose. That means that your entire life—all of it—is meant to serve him, to brag about him, to honor and point to him. Your life, your body, your emotions, and your actions all were designed for one purpose: his glory.

When you find the purpose of your life, you want nothing more than to commit yourself to that purpose. In Romans 12:1–2 you can see how this consecrating of your life begins. Paul writes,

> I appeal to you therefore, brothers, by the mercies of God, to present your bodies as a living sacrifice, holy and acceptable to God, which is your spiritual worship. Do not be conformed to this world, but be transformed by the renewal of your mind, that by testing you may

discern what is the will of God, what is good and acceptable and perfect.

Your life is meant to be a living sacrifice—a walking, talking sacrifice that gives up all claims to the things you used to hold dear and obsesses over God and God alone. When you decide to set yourself apart for one purpose, his glory, your other obsessions lose their power over you. The call that used to draw you to them now sounds harsh and destructive, and you want nothing to do with it. As you start to see that denying yourself—sacrificing the things your heart currently craves in order to learn to crave God more fully—sets you free from the chains of this world, you will become more and more devoted, more and more obsessed with God, and less interested in the stuff you used to think about and yearn for.

Life

We all live for something. The fashionista lives for fashion. The actor lives for applause. The surgeon lives for healing. The couch potato lives for good television. The God Girl lives for God. **When you obsess over God, you**

give up your right to yourself. You say no to your desire to find glory in anything other than him, and instead you choose to live for him. After all, you reason with the apostle Paul, "he died for all, that those who live might no longer live for themselves but for him who for their sake died and was raised" (2 Cor. 5:15). When you live for yourself you die, because your self cannot sustain you; it cannot protect you, comfort you, or save you. **Those who live for themselves believe they are serving themselves when really they are damaging themselves.**

Study

The obsessed spend all their energy getting to know their obsession. The athlete watches game tapes, studies the plays, and gets to know the sport inside out. She has one goal: to be a better athlete. Because of that, she studies. She knows that without study she can't succeed at her obsession. **Obsession requires study of the material**; it requires attention to the craft of your obsession, and that goes for faith too. When you are God-obsessed, you are ravenous for more of him. You want to know what makes him tick, what he loves, and what he hates. You want to be in the know.

How do you become more God-obsessed? By becoming more mindful of his love for you and what that love has driven him to do. If you don't know enough to love him to the point of obsession, then find out more about the love of God in his Word. Read it, devour it, hide it in your heart, and you'll feed your obsession. The more you focus on something, the more it comes into your thoughts, and the more you give your attention to something, the more obsessed you become. So feed your God-obsession with more of his Word.

Truth

When you are obsessed with something, you talk about it a lot, don't you? And when it's something you think is important or even essential for others, you will stand up for what you obsess over in order to bring others into your obsession. This model fits your God-obsession. God's Word feeds the life of faith. His very words to us, found in the Bible, are paramount in the life of faith and in the salvation of the world. God has entrusted you with his Word, given it to you for yourself but also for others. He wants you to stand up for the truth of his Word and not to let others who claim to know him live in deception or teach what isn't true. In Jude 3 you are called to "contend for the faith." That means that when God is assaulted, when lies are being told, when the truth isn't taught, the obsessed say something about it. They stand up for truth. This proves their obsession not with pleasing people or self but with living in the truth of God's Word and standing up for it when others step outside of that truth.

Praise

Obsession drives you to praise. For example, the person obsessed with food talks about the food they love a lot and praises the good stuff on their plate. When you are obsessed with love, how much do you praise the object of your love? Love prompts praise and thanksgiving. The same is true of your love for God: it drives you to praise him, to talk about his greatness, to thank him for all he is, and to tell others about what he has done. In your praise you glorify God (see Ps. 86:12).

Telling Others

Obsession leads to boasting. Whatever you think about the most will fill most of your conversation. When you are obsessed with God, your conversations focus on telling others about him. This doesn't just mean other nonbelievers but includes believers as well. How many of us know God's truth but fall into temptation out of ignorance or self-deception? When someone knows God but acts like they don't, they need the loving words of a sister (or brother) to remind them of the God they serve.

Telling others about God is a symptom of a God-obsession. When he's everything you think about and you see someone in need of him, you can't help but offer a gentle reminder of who he is. If they have never met him before, then your words are even more important. Telling others about the saving grace of Jesus Christ will fuel your obsession as you see how his love changes lives.

Suffering

In this world you are going to suffer. There is no way out of it. As Jesus said, "In the world you will have tribulation. But take heart; I have overcome the world" (John 16:33). When you trust God with your suffering, you glorify him. **Your suffering is important in your life and the life of others.** When you suffer well you point others to God. You prove his faithfulness and presence in your life. If you want to be God-obsessed, then find out the value of suffering. Look into his Word and see the beauty that comes from the fire of trials (see Matt. 5:11–12; Rom. 5:3–4; 2 Cor. 4:17–18). Look at what suffering can do for a life obsessed not with self but with the One who is worthy.

Your heart will be restless, your mind tortured, and your life controlled until you find your obsession in God. No other obsession will satisfy you, serve you, or save you. In fact, all other obsessions ultimately destroy you. When you obsess over anything or anyone other than God, you misplace your worship and turn your back on God. But when you obsess over God, your entire life gets put into perspective. What used to hurt you now improves you. What used to scare you now teaches you. The weakness you used to live with is now your strength. To obsess is your very nature; it's no wonder you've found so many avenues for obsession. But the life of Christ in you is there to change your nature by giving you a new nature (see 2 Cor. 5:17). As you obsess over the life of Christ in you, this new nature softens the blows of life and gives you hope where you used to see darkness.

To be God-obsessed is to break free from the things of this world that consume you and to live for truth, to live for freedom, and to live for love. The God-obsessed see God in all of their circumstances, and because of that nothing can ever truly harm them, because they have so much trust in his gentle and loving hand. As a God Girl, your obsession defines you. Don't let the words "freak" or "loser" distract you from the glory that comes from a life bent on serving God. What others see as weakness, you know to be power.

But before you can obsess over God, you must determine to love him with all of your heart, not just a part. You must decide to give him all of your thoughts, not just some. You must dedicate all of your strength to him, not save some for yourself. And you must give him all of your soul, not only a portion. When you do this it will all come back to you and more, as all of your heart will then be able to love others with God's love. All of your thoughts will serve others better when you share the mind and will of God. Your strength will be more than it ever was when it was divided between God and this world. And in the end your soul will be satisfied and free.

Refuse to obsess over anything in this world. Direct all your obsession upward. Give all your life to Christ. Turn it over and refuse to devote it to anything else, and you will be God-obsessed.

To be God-obsessed
is to break free from the things
of this world that consume you

and to live for truth,
to live for freedom,
and to live for love.

Notes

1. Bodie Hodge, "How Long Did It Take for Noah to Build the Ark?" AnswersinGenesis.org, June 1, 2010, http://www.answers ingenesis.org/articles/2010/06/01/long-to-build-the-ark.

2. "Hudson Taylor: Faith Missionary to China," ChristianHis tory.net, August 8, 2008, http://www.christianitytoday.com/ch/131christians/missionaries/htaylor.html.

3. A. W. Tozer, *The Knowledge of the Holy* (New York: Harper-One, 1978), 15.

4. Quoted in Darrel W. Amundsen, "The Anguish and Agonies of Charles Spurgeon," *Christian History* 29 (1991), 25.

5. Ibid.

Hayley DiMarco is the bestselling and award-winning author or coauthor of over thirty books, including *God Girl*, the *God Girl Bible*, *Mean Girls*, *Over It*, and *Die Young*. She and her husband, Michael, run Hungry Planet, a company focused on producing books that combine hard-hitting biblical truth with cutting-edge design. They live in Nashville, Tennessee.

Obsessed with Obsessed?

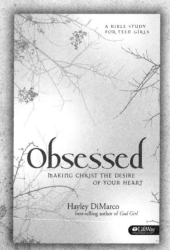

A BIBLE STUDY FOR TEEN GIRLS

Obsessed

MAKING CHRIST THE DESIRE OF YOUR HEART

Hayley DiMarco
best-selling author of *God Girl*

Share it with friends.

Continue to confront what's consuming you with Hayley's six-week Bible study.

Obsessed: Making Christ the Desire of Your Heart

Find it at:
lifeway.com /girls
LifeWay Christian Stores
800.458.2772

Hungry Planet Helps Girls Become the Women They Are Meant to Be

When you become a God Girl, your life will never be the same.

Available Wherever Books Are Sold

Revell
a division of Baker Publishing Group
www.RevellBooks.com

www.hungryplanet.net

You're on the path to becoming a God Girl. Here's a daily map to guide each step.

A 365-day devotional that offers teen girls a daily resource for deepening their relationship with God through a personal quiet time.

Available Wherever Books Are Sold
Also Available in Ebook Format

Revell
a division of Baker Publishing Group
www.RevellBooks.com

Hungry Planet
www.hungryplanet.net

GodGirl.com

The *Ultimate Bible* just for the *God Girl!*

It's a blank canvas—design your own cover! Download patterns and stencils at GodGirl.com.

With special features like Ask Yourself, Prayers, God Girl Stories, and Know This Devotions, all written by bestselling author Hayley DiMarco, the *God Girl Bible* is a must-have for girls thirteen and up! If you're ready to grow closer to God, grow in your faith, and join an on-line group of girls from around the globe growing together, the *God Girl Bible* is for you!

Available Wherever Books Are Sold

Revell
a division of Baker Publishing Group
www.RevellBooks.com

Hungry Planet
www.hungryplanet.net

GodGirl.com

At GodGirl.com, you can be mentored by bestselling author Hayley DiMarco in what it means to be a God Girl and get help with the challenges of life in the process.

Here are just some of the features of GodGirl.com:

- Free books, resources, and an online Bible to grow in your relationship with God.
- God Girl Academy is a four-part spiritual mentoring course you can go through on your own or as part of a group.
- Quick Relief section gives you Bible verses organized by the topics you need at the moment.
- Exclusive live online events with Hayley and her friends.
- Design Your Own GG Bible cover hints and templates for the one and only all-white blank canvas God Girl Bible.
- And much, much more!

And if you're a leader of a small group, you can use GodGirl.com as a meeting hub and resource library full of tools for discipleship and mentoring young women.

WHAT DO YOU FEAR?

Failure? Bullies? Pop quizzes? Abandonment? Natural disasters? Doing something embarrassing?

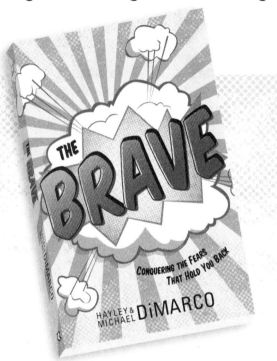

There's a ton of stuff in this world that makes us fearful, stressed, and worried. Things that make us want to give up and hide. Things that make us doubt that God cares. But the Brave around us aren't somehow superhuman. They've just learned to have faith. Not in themselves, but in something—in Someone—much bigger than their fears. It might be easier than you think.

Available Wherever Books Are Sold
Also Available in Ebook Format